FOR JAMES

ON HIS SIXTH BIRTHDAY

with love from Mummy and Daddy.

19th August 1981.

SIMPLE HERALDRY

CHEERFULLY ILLUSTRATED

This edition completely revised
and updated 1978

© Sir Iain Moncreiffe of that Ilk
BT., O.ST.J., PH.D., F.S.A.
Advocate, Albany Herald of Arms
and
Don Pottinger, O.ST.J., M.A. (HONS). D.A.
Unicorn Pursuivant of Arms

Pottinger, Don
Simple heraldry. - 2nd ed. revised.
1. Heraldry - History
I. Title   II. Moncrieffe, *Sir* Iain, *bart*
929.6'09   CR151

ISBN 0-7028-1009-6

This revised edition published 1978 by

John Bartholomew & Son Limited,
12 Duncan Street, Edinburgh, EH9 1TA.
and at 216 High Street, Bromley BR1 1PW.

Printed in Great Britain by

John Bartholomew & Son Ltd, Edinburgh

SIMPLE HERALDRY

BY

SIR IAIN MONCREIFFE OF THAT ILK
BT., O.ST.J., PH.D., F.SA., ADVOCATE,
ALBANY HERALD OF ARMS

AND

DON POTTINGER. O.ST.J., M.A.(HONS). D.A.
UNICORN PURSUIVANT OF ARMS

JOHN BARTHOLOMEW AND SON LIMITED
EDINBURGH AND LONDON

PREFACE

  Heraldry, the floral border in the garden of history, is of its very nature colourful and gay. But it is not just a border of the tallest tulips with a background of ancient laurels : a picturesque record of the achievements and courage of past leaders of the people. It is also part of the flowered pageantry that brightens the living present for the ordinary man. He may not own his own "trademark" or coat of arms—though there is often no reason why he should not, as he will find later in this book—but he certainly belongs to a nation, and probably also to some club, Service unit or other organisation, which does bear arms. For heraldry symbolises communities as well as individual men.

There has been a tremendous revival of interest in heraldry during the last two decades. Lyon Clerk tells us that more new coats of arms have been registered in Scotland since 1930 than in the previous three hundred years—while in England an ever-widening group belongs to the new Heraldry Society founded by Mr J. P. Brooke-Little. Our simple guide is therefore intended to be instructive as well as cheerful.

It is difficult to be brief about so wide a subject without generalising. But our guide would lack simplicity if we invariably tried to safeguard ourselves from captious pedants by qualifying general statements almost to the point of ambiguity. Scholarship requires that we should now add the usual warning that there may be exceptions to any general rule. Thus there are no heraldic rules about shades of colour—any blue is *azure* to a herald. The exception to this rule is the rare sky-blue or *bleu celeste* of some Continental armorists.

For the sake of brevity, we have often given the owner's surname alone or simplest style, when depicting a coat of arms belonging to the head of an historic family. Similarly, since there are no strict conventions about the artistic treatment of heraldic devices, we have tried in practice to use the simplest forms of outline. We have also tended to omit details such as crests and mantlings irrelevant to the particular points illustrated, and a number of conventionalised anachronisms in costume have been found convenient. Thus we depict knights at Flodden in chain-mail instead of plate armour. But our illustrations are not all as fanciful as some may perhaps seem. For example, an armorial elephant rug (see p. 25) was actually to be seen at the Heraldic Exhibition which we organised in Edinburgh for the 1951 Festival.

Of course it has not been possible to cram everything into this short book. For instance, we had no space to say that an *orle* is the hem of a coat of arms—that a *bezant* is a gold roundel—that a *fountain* is a roundel of blue and white waves (see p. 24)—or that in England the Sovereign is the only woman to have a crest, though a few great Scots heiresses are allowed them. Nor could we mention the Scots practice of "nomination", whereby arms may be specially settled on any line chosen from "the Blood and Name", subject to Lyon's approval. Also, there was little room in Part Five to interpret the Norman-French (with a touch of Saracen) that was used in blazon by Western chivalry—and still less for the many technical refinements of modern heraldry, to which Sir Christopher and Adrian Lynch-Robinson's *Intelligible Heraldry* serves as an introduction.

There are many books in which our readers can widen their knowledge. They should certainly start with the late Oswald Barron's masterpiece on Heraldry in the *Encyclopædia Britannica, 11th ed.* Other books include Sir Anthony Wagner's *Heraldry in England* and his later invaluable works; J.P. Brooke-Little's revised editions of *Boutell's Heraldry* and Fox-Davies's *Complete Guide to Heraldry;* Sir Thomas Innes of Learney's *Scots Heraldry;* Sir Francis Grant's *Manual of Heraldry*, and for reference, besides *Debrett* and *Burke,* the standard reprints of Papworth's *Ordinary of British Armorials*, Burke's *General Armory* (supplemented by C.R. Humphery-Smith's *General Armory Two)*, Fairbairn's *Book of Crests* and Elvin's *A Dictionary of Heraldry.*

However, there are now so many able writers on heraldry that those who are interested would be wise to join the *Heraldry Society,* 28 Museum Street, London WC1A 1LH, take its quarterly magazine 'The Coat of Arms', and consult its officials. The *Heraldry Society of Scotland* (c/o Charles J. Burnett, 1 Queen Street, Edinburgh EH2 1JD) also publishes a newsletter, 'The Double Tressure'. From these bodies can be obtained the current address of such fellow institutions as the *Canadian Heraldry Society, Heraldry Society of New Zealand, American College of Heraldry, Scandinavian Heraldry Society* and the *Commonwealth Heraldry Board.*

ACKNOWLEDGEMENTS

reprinted from the original edition

Our warmest thanks are given both to Sir Thomas Innes of Learney, Lord Lyon King of Arms, who is the unrivalled authority on Scots heraldry, and to Mr Anthony R. Wagner, Richmond Herald, who has been described as "the best scholar in the College of Arms since Camden", for doing us the great honour of reading through our MS and making invaluable suggestions.

For particular points of heraldic detail we are indebted to Lt.-Colonel H. A. B. Lawson, Rothesay Herald ; the Master of Sinclair, Portcullis Pursuivant ; Mr Michael Maclagan, Slains Pursuivant ; Mr Hugh Stanford London, F.S.A. ; and Miss Anne E. Simson, Secretary to the Lord Lyon.

For points of illustrative detail or other helpful suggestions we would also like to thank the Duke of Atholl ; Lord Perth ; Admiral Sir Angus Cunninghame Graham ; Colonel H. Carkeet-James, Resident Governor and Major of the Tower of London ; Colonel G. C. Gordon-Lennox, Lieutenant-Colonel Commanding Grenadier Guards, with his Regimental Adjutant, Major the Honble. Neville Wigram, and Assistant Adjutant, Major John Wiggin ; Major H. P. E. Pereira, Curator of the Scottish United Services Museum—and three Knights of the Sovereign and Military Order of Malta : the Captain of Dunstaffnage (Angus John Campbell), the Keeper of Falkland (Major Michael Crichton-Stuart) and the Honble. Charles Stourton.

A Knight of another Order of Chivalry, to whom we are also indebted for a point of illustrative detail, is America's unofficial ambassador of goodwill : Commander Douglas Fairbanks, Jnr., whose arms appropriately symbolise the two hemispheres united across the blue Atlantic by the silken knot of friendship. Indeed, the modern upsurge of enthusiasm for our colourful science owes much to the interest shown in heraldry by Americans, many of whom have recently recorded arms of their own in the United Kingdom.

CONTENTS

FOR

DIANA AND FAY

PART ONE

ARMS AND THE MAN

HIS COAT OF ARMS

A man in full armour was unrecognisable.

So each man wore a distinctive coat, by which he could be recognised, over his armour. This was called his coat "of arms".

These "arms" were displayed on his banner, shield and horsecloth, as well as on his coat—

and came to be worn in civil life too.

As no two men in the same region could wear exactly the same coat of arms, these "arms" were soon used separately as personal symbols—and especially to mark their owners' possessions, because few people could read in those days. Such a coat of arms is usually depicted on a shield.

Coat of arms of Drummond

HIS HELMET AND CREST

A personal "crest" of light wood or boiled leather came to be worn—like a cock's comb—on top of the helmet.

Below the crest a silken mantle hung down to keep the heat of the sun off the back of the armour.

This "mantling" was kept in place by a wreath of twisted silk.

Some great men wore a "chapeau" or a crest-coronet instead of the wreath.

Crest of Drummond

Helmet, crest and mantling are usually depicted above the shield.

With the addition of a motto on a scroll, this forms the normal heraldic "achievement" of an ordinary gentleman.

HIS BADGE

The crest is often depicted for convenience on the wreath alone, without the helmet, as a mark of ownership.

In Scotland, a metal plate showing a chief's crest and motto used to be suspended by a strap and buckle around the necks of his retainers.

So nowadays a chief's crest, when encircled by a strap and buckle bearing his motto, may be worn as a badge by all his staff and family or clan.

Crest-badge of Drummond

Many chiefs have plant-badges as well, which may also be worn by their clan.

Plant-badge of Drummond

A small shield of the arms was worn as a badge in some countries, and a number of great men have other heraldic badges—used to mark their property and to distinguish their followers.

Caltrap, badge of Drummond

Sleuth-hound, badge of Drummond

How Drummond got the caltrap for his badge

HIS WHOLE ACHIEVEMENT

T hese badges are sometimes displayed on a background of the "liveries" (usually the two principal tinctures of the shield), on a headquarters flag called the "standard".

Drummond, Earl of Perth

All peers, and those Scots lairds who are territorial barons, may place a chapeau above their shields—peers always put it inside their coronets.

Mantlings are normally of the livery colours, but the Sovereign's is gold, lined with ermine, and those of Scots peers and certain Officers of State are red, lined with ermine.

Certain prominent men are also allowed to depict their shields held up by "supporters", which stand on a mound called a "compartment".

So the full achievement of a peer is made up of his coat of arms, chapeau, coronet, helmet, crest, mantling, motto, supporters, and compartment.

Achievement of Drummond Earl of Perth

HIS USE OF HERALDRY

His heraldic emblems can be used in innumerable ways to mark his property.

They can appear on such things as curtains, furniture,

brushes, cuff-links, buttons, brooches, silver, china and writing paper.

They are also used to identify him. Scotsmen wear their own personal crest or their chief's crest-badge in their bonnets (chiefs add three eagle's feathers and chieftains two).

Livery colours are often used, especially as Racing Colours.

He can fly his banner over his house, and on his motor car.

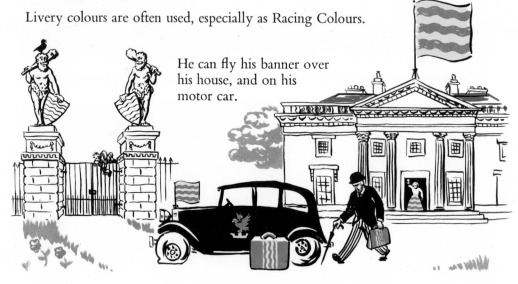

PART TWO

ARMS AND THE FAMILY

WIVES AND DAUGHTERS

Daughters are allowed by courtesy to use their fathers' coats, which they conventionally depict on a diamond-shaped "lozenge".

When they marry, they place their own family coat beside their husband's, on his shield.
This is called "impaling".

If their father has no sons, they become heraldic heiresses when he dies. Then they may place their own family shield in the middle of their husband's shield, and it is called an "escutcheon of pretence".

Drummond

Hay

Talbot

*Nevill,
Lord
Furnival*

ELDEST SONS

Because no two men may wear the same coat of arms simultaneously, even the eldest son must use a special mark during his father's lifetime.

This mark is called a "label".

Old Talbot, 1st Earl of Shrewsbury

(In Scotland, this mark may be used by whoever is next in succession to the coat of arms).

Young Talbot, his eldest son

When his father dies, he inherits the plain coat of arms from him, and removes the label.

Young Talbot, 2nd Earl of Shrewsbury

OTHER SONS

Younger sons and their descendants had to make some permanent change in their fathers' arms.

This is called "differencing".

Sometimes they changed the colours—

sometimes they added new devices to the coat—

or a border—

or both. **O**r else they combined it with another coat.

But branches living in separate countries were not always compelled to "difference" the original coat.

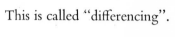

*HAY
Earl of
Erroll*

*Lord Hay,
eldest son
of Erroll*

*Lord Hay
of Yester*

*Hay of
Park*

*Hay in
Leith*

*Hay of
Hayfield*

*Haye, sire de
la Haye Hue
[in Normandy]*

*Hay of
Leys*

*Hay of
Broxmouth*

*Hay of
Boyne*

*Hay of
Fudie*

*Hay of
Naughton*

*Hay, Earl
of Kinnoull*

*Hay of
Slade
[in Ireland]*

*Hay, Earl
of Carlisle
[in England]*

NATURAL CHILDREN

Right side

Wrong side

Campbell, Duke of Argyll

William Campbell, Bastard of Argyll

I n Scotland, natural children are entitled to arms by right, but are given special marks of difference.

I n England, they have to seek a new grant of arms from the Crown. This may be either the original coat with a special mark of difference, or an entirely new coat, often alluding to the father's.

Badge of Stanley

Sir John Stanley, Bastard of Derby

Stanley, Earl of Derby

Like other differences, these marks are retained by descendants. So a man who has such a mark on his coat is not necessarily illegitimate himself.

King of France

de St. Remi de Valois, Bastard of France

ENGLISH CHILDREN

William Nevill,
Earl of Kent

I n England, there has been since Tudor times a regular system of differencing the coats of arms of younger sons.

Ralph Nevill,
Earl of
Westmorland

It consists of a special mark for each legitimate son in order of birth. The eldest son has his label. The second son has a crescent, the third a star, the fourth a bird called a "martlet", the fifth a ring, the sixth a fleur-de-lys, the seventh a rose, the eighth a certain kind of Cross called a "Cross moline", and the ninth an eight-petalled flower. These marks may be of any heraldic tincture.

Thomas Nevill,
Lord Furnival

his eldest son,
John,
Lord Nevill

George Nevill,
Lord Latimer

The eldest son drops his label on succeeding to the family coat. But the younger sons retain their individual marks, and pass them on to their descendants—whose younger sons in turn add further differences.

Edward Nevill,
Lord Bergavenny

SCOTTISH CHILDREN

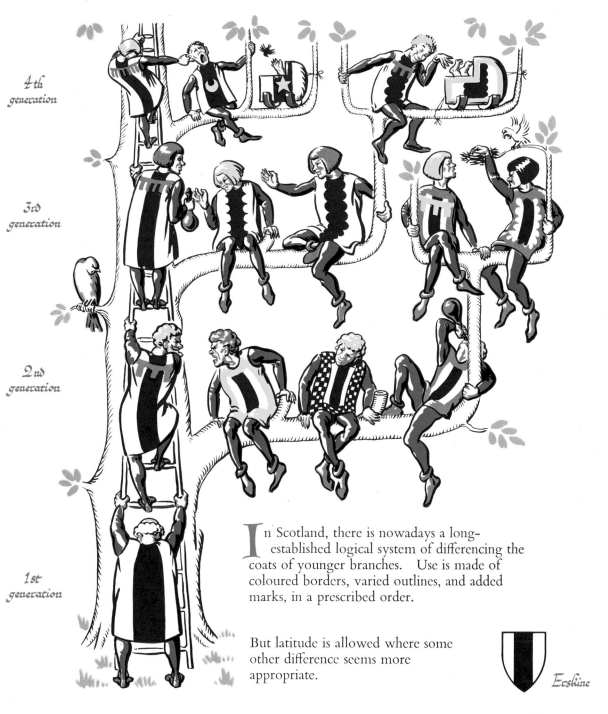

In Scotland, there is nowadays a long-established logical system of differencing the coats of younger branches. Use is made of coloured borders, varied outlines, and added marks, in a prescribed order.

But latitude is allowed where some other difference seems more appropriate.

Ersline

21

HEIRS

I n the Middle Ages coats of arms were often passed down in the same way as land. Thus if a man had no sons, his property—land and arms alike —passed to his daughter and then to her son.

Bagot

Stafford

This is still a Scottish practice, but for many centuries any Scotsman who succeeds to a coat of arms through his mother has had to take her surname alone if he wants to be allowed the plain coat.

O therwise he cannot use a coat inherited through his mother unless he "quarters" it with his father's coat— and indeed this has been the only method normally allowed in England since at least Tudor times. "Quartering" takes place when a shield is divided into equal "quarters", in which are placed the various coats of arms its owner has inherited.

Bowes

Lyon

Of course if a man with no sons had several daughters, all his grandchildren could eventually "quarter" his arms with their own fathers' coats.

Bowes — Lyon

MORE HEIRS

Several generations of marriages to heiresses can bring a large number of "quarterings" into a family.

They are still called "quarterings" even when there are more than four of them.

Fraser

Up to four coats may be placed one in each quarter of the shield (vacant quarters being filled by repetitions).

Keith

Drummond

Above this number, the four quarters of the shield may become "grand quarters", one or more of them being sub-divided into lesser quarters to accommodate the extra coats.

Elphinstone

"Grand quartering" is still the rule in Scotland (where a convenient selection of the more significant quarterings may be made by official authority, sometimes omitting the coats of intervening heiresses).

Fullerton

Buller

Lord Elphinstone

23

In England, since Tudor times, any number of new coats may be added to the shield consecutively without sub-division into fours. A shield then becomes "quarterly of six" or "quarterly of ten", or whatever the number of coats may be.

Stourton

Le Moyne

Belvale

Chideock

Fitz Payn

Fitz Warin

Argentine

Fauntleroy

Howard

Mowbray

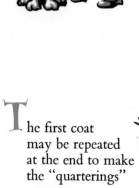

The first coat may be repeated at the end to make the "quarterings" up to an even number.

Segrave

Plantagenet of Norfolk

Fitzalan

Warenne

Dacre

Greystoke

Talbot

Cummin

Baliol

Galloway

S o many quarterings can be accumulated by an old English family during several centuries that a quarterly coat sometimes becomes so large that it would almost require an elephant to carry it.

It is not necessary to show all the accumulated quarterings, provided that junior branches show any which they use as differences to their plain family coat (where they have "differenced by quartering").

For convenience, only about half a dozen quarterings are usually shown.

But if a quartering is shown which has descended through more than one woman, then the coats of all *intervening* heiresses must also be shown.

Lord Mowbray and Stourton

25

SAME NAME

H aving the same surname does not entitle a man to use another's arms.

If he can prove a blood relationship he is entitled to a differenced version of those arms. But he may be unable to prove it—or may not be related at all, in which case he has no right whatever to any form of those arms.

Thomas B. Browne

I n England, therefore, unrelated families who happen to have the same surname are usually given utterly dissimilar plain coats of arms.

Alexander Browne

B ut in clannish Scotland, where plain arms are the mark of a Chief, there can be only one Chief of any surname—and so any man who bears (or takes) that surname comes beneath that Chief's banner.   He is therefore only granted arms which allude in some way to those of his Chief.

Gordon of Huntly, the Chief

But such coats are quite unlike the systematically differenced coats of proved branches of the Chief's house.

Robert Gordon, stranger

Gordon of Pitlurg, branch of chief's house

PART THREE

ARMS AND THE PEOPLE

COMMUNITIES

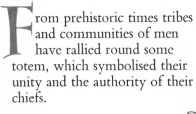

From prehistoric times tribes and communities of men have rallied round some totem, which symbolised their unity and the authority of their chiefs.

White Horse of the Saxons

"Eagle" of ancient Rome

At the dawn of heraldry the tendency to have such symbols became standardised in the use of public arms by communities as such.

Holy Roman Empire

Hanover

REALMS

King of England

I n monarchies, the arms of the realm are the arms of its monarch, who is the living symbol of his people.

Holy Roman Emperor

King of Scots

Duke of Bavaria

Such arms are called "Arms of Dominion".

Holy Roman Empire

Hapsburg

Prince of Wales

New dynasties almost always abandon their family arms and assume those of the realm.

Landgrave of Hesse

Count of Flanders

Arms of Dominion mark the public authority of the Crown, and must not be used by private citizens.

Hapsburg, Holy Roman Emperor

29

FIEFS

Isle of Man

Stanley

Stanley, Sovereign Lord of Man

O ccasionally dynasties retain their family coats, and combine them with their Arms of Dominion. But this is more often done by the holders of great territorial fiefs.

Sometimes they quarter their family coat with the arms of their fief—

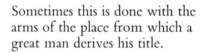

sometimes they place one coat on a smaller shield in the middle of the other—

sometimes they do both, when they have more than one fief.

Stewart of Darnley

Seigneurie d'Aubigny

Earldom of Lennox

Stewart of Darnley, Earl of Lennox, Seigneur d'Aubigny

Sometimes this is done with the arms of the place from which a great man derives his title.

City of Edinburgh

Duke of Edinburgh

NATIONS

"Union Jack"

St. Andrew's Cross

St. Patrick's Cross

St. George's Cross

The Dannebrog

Belgian Flag

Polish Flag

King of Poland, afterwards Republic of Poland

King of the Belgians

Monarchs also possess special badge-flags, flown by their subjects as tokens of their allegiance and as marks of national identity.

These National Flags are often derived from the Cross of a Patron Saint, from some other royal badge, or from the livery colours of the Sovereign's own Arms of Dominion.

31

REPUBLICS

Florence

Switzerland

Ancient Republics have had their own arms since early times. These are their marks of public authority.

More recent Republics often continue to use the Arms of Dominion of their former rulers.

Flag of Austrian Republic

Archduke of Austria

Or they take new arms—
perhaps alluding to a national hero—

Flag of U.S.A.

Shield of U.S.A.

George Washington

Turkey

sometimes adopting religious or ideological symbols.

U.S.S.R.

TOWNS AND DISTRICTS

Towns also have arms of their own, which are the symbols of their corporate identity and municipal authority.

City of London

City of Leeds

So do territorial districts, whose arms are used by the County Council or other administrative body.

Province of Leinster

Lancashire County Council

Northumberland County Council

These arms are often based on those of the historic local lord.

Burgh of Grantown-on-Spey

Grant, Lord Strathspey

COMPANIES

Worshipful Company of Cutlers of London

Within the towns, trades associations developed from the old guilds into noble Livery Companies with their own arms and heraldic liveries. Some great merchant companies spread far beyond the towns, administering wide territories under their Livery Flags.

Worshipful Company of Girdlers of London

Livery Flag of the Honourable East India Company

Hudson's Bay Company

Honourable East India Company

34

OTHER CORPORATE BODIES

Many other corporate bodies have arms of their own. For instance, arms have been granted to such varied institutions as schools, banks, abbeys, hospitals, fire brigades, masonic lodges, universities, national and regional boards, business firms, clubs and other societies.

Bank of Scotland

Crichton Royal Mental Institution

The Royal Society

British Broadcasting Corporation

Deeside Field Club

Queen's Park Football Club

Oxford University

Lanark Fire Brigade

Corporation of Lloyd's

Butley Priory

These bodies use their arms to mark their property just as private individuals do. They appear as their flags, and also as their distinguishing marks on anything from college blazers and whisky bottles to wrought-iron gates and writing paper.

Heriot's School

Eton College

OFFICIALS

The heads of institutions often "impale" their own personal arms with those of the institutions—

as though they are "married" to them (the institution occupying the husband's position on the shield).

Other arms that go with appointments may be combined by the holders with their personal arms.

Bishopric of Durham

Robert Nevill

Robert Nevill, Bishop of Durham

Edward Hawkins

Oriel College

Edward Hawkins, Provost of Oriel

Hereditary Butler of Ireland

Marquess of Ormonde

Ormonde, Butler of Ireland

Arch-Chamberlain of the Holy Roman Empire

Margrave of Brandenburg

Brandenburg, Arch-Chamberlain

PART FOUR

ARMS AND
THE CROWN

ROYAL ARMS

Kingdom of England

Kingdom of Ireland

Our present Queen reigns over us because Her Majesty is a direct descendant of the mighty Sovereigns of England and Ireland—and of the ancient Kings of Scots, the oldest continuing dynasty in Christendom.

Kingdom of Scotland

United Kingdom

Her Majesty therefore quarters the historic coats of these kingdoms.

These coats are the Queen's exclusive property, and none of them may ever be used except by Her Majesty's authority.

Personal Flag of the Sovereign

The quarterly coat is flown as the personal flag of the Sovereign as such, and marks Her Majesty's presence.

The Royal Arms are arranged rather differently in England and in Scotland, giving greater prominence in each country to its own national elements.

Royal Arms as used in England

DIEU ET MON DROIT

Royal Arms as used in Scotland

IN DEFENS

NEMO ME IMPUNE LACESSIT

ROYAL BADGES

The Queen possesses a number of royal badges.

Some are used to mark Crown property, and others are worn by Her Majesty's subjects as a token of their allegiance.

The national flags are themselves royal badges.

Badge of England

Badge of Wales

The Union Badge

England

There are also royal plant badges for each nation in the British Isles—

and many other local royal badges.

Scotland

Wales

Badges of Ireland

The United Kingdom

Imperial Crown

Perhaps the royal badges most widely used throughout the Commonwealth and Empire are the Crown itself, and the Royal Cypher, the Sovereign's crowned initials.

Royal Cypher

ROYAL CONSORTS

Queen Ann Nevill

Queen Margaret Drummond

When the Sovereign is a King, his consort as Queen impales the Royal Arms with those of her own family, in the ordinary way.

Queen Elizabeth [Bowes-Lyon] now the Queen Mother

When Lord Darnley married Mary, Queen of Scots, he became King Consort as "Henry, King of Scots". Queen Mary Tudor's husband was already a King ; and Mary II's husband, William of Orange, became King as William III. But the husbands of Queen Anne and Queen Victoria retained instead their title of Prince.

Albert, Prince Consort

Prince Albert, as Prince Consort, quartered the British Royal Arms (differenced by a special label) with his own Saxon royal coat.

Saxony

Prince Albert's Label

Denmark

The Duke of Edinburgh belongs to the same great royal family as the present Kings of Denmark, Greece and Norway.

Edinburgh

Greece

Mountbatten

With the royal arms of Denmark and Greece (his father's family), His Royal Highness quarters the arms of Mountbatten (his mother's famous family) —and also those of the royal city of Edinburgh, from which the Duke derives his title.

Duke of Edinburgh

ROYAL FAMILY

Duke of Cornwall and Rothesay

Prince of Wales

Prince Charles, as Heir Apparent to the Throne, is automatically Duke of Cornwall in England by descent from the Plantagenets—and also Duke of Rothesay and Prince and Steward of Scotland by descent from the Stewarts, Earl of Carrick by descent from Robert the Bruce, and Lord of the Isles (he is descended from an heiress of Somerled, King of the Isles).   The first Duke of Cornwall was the Black Prince. His Royal Highness differences the Royal Arms with a plain white label, and possesses the famous badge of ostrich plumes.

Badge of the Heir Apparent

When the Heir Apparent is created Prince of Wales he places the arms of Wales in the centre of his shield.

Earl of Kent, 5th son of Edward I

Formerly, younger sons of the Royal Family used various differences ; and married daughters of the Sovereign impaled the plain royal arms with their husband's coat.

Lady Erroll, daughter of Robert II

Duke of Gloucester

But for many centuries now all members of the Royal Family have had differenced versions of the Royal Arms settled on them by Royal Warrant.

Duke of Windsor

Duke of Kent

They are always given white labels, of three or five points, on which each prince or princess has individual marks to form his or her particular difference.

These are given to royal princesses as well as to royal princes.

Princess Margaret

41

HER MAJESTY'S DOMINIONS

Apart from the Royal Arms, which are the symbol of the Sovereign everywhere, bearings have been assigned to Her Majesty's Governments in the great Dominions, for use as marks of public authority there.

Canada

With the famous maple leaves—and the arms of England, Scotland and Ireland—the bearings of Canada include, for the French Canadians, the royal arms of France.

The Queen is descended from the old Kings of France, the line of Saint Louis.

Australia

The Australian bearings symbolise the six states that form the Commonwealth of Australia —and those of South Africa symbolise the four provinces of the Union.

South Africa

New Zealand

As with Australia, the stars of the Southern Cross appear in the bearings of New Zealand —and regional allusions also occur in the bearings of Ceylon.

Ceylon

Ensign of Australia

Her Majesty also possesses badges in each Dominion which, when placed with the Union Badge on a blue ensign, are "worn" by ships in public employment—and on a red ensign, are flown by citizens on their own ships as marks of national identity.

Merchant Flag of New Zealand

HER MAJESTY'S SERVANTS

Royal Arms

Royal Cypher Badge

The Civil Service and other employees of the Crown make extensive use, in Her Majesty's name, of the Royal Arms and Badges.

Imperial Crown Badge

Of these, perhaps the badge most in use is the Imperial Crown itself.

Imperial Crown Badge

Royal Plant Badges

Some servants of the Queen, such as the Yeomen Warders of the Tower, still wear the royal plant-badges on breast and back in mediæval manner.

The continuing use by certain Crown departments of the badge of Sidney (the broad-arrow) is a relic of the service of a Sidney, who as Master of the Ordnance nearly three centuries ago used his personal badge to mark the stores for which he was responsible.

Badge of Sidney

Most of the coinage struck by Her Majesty's Mint bears the Royal Arms, Crests or Badges.

Royal Arms

Royal Crest of England

Royal Crest of Scotland

Royal Plant Badges

43

HER MAJESTY'S FORCES

ROYAL NAVY

White Ensign

Her Majesty possesses a special badge-flag for use by royal ships of war (and by the Royal Yacht Squadron). This is the famous White Ensign.

Admiralty Flag

The gold anchor, formerly badge of the Lord High Admiral, is still borne by the Board of Admiralty.

Naval Crown

Badge of H.M.S. Renown

Her Majesty's ships have individual badges of their own, surrounded by a rope beneath a "naval crown".

ROYAL AIR FORCE

Her Majesty's aircraft bear roundels of the livery colours of the Union.

Astral Crown

Badge of Fighter Command, Royal Air Force

Formations have their own individual badges, prepared for them by a herald who is Inspector of Royal Air Force Badges, and approved by the Queen in person.

The frames of these badges are different for each Dominion.

Badge of 6 Squadron, Royal Australian Air Force

44

HER MAJESTY'S FORCES
THE ARMY

Mackenzie of Seaforth

Cap badge of the Seaforth Highlanders

R egimental badges are worn on caps, collars and buttons. They often allude to the man who raised the regiment, its territorial connection, its function or its battle honours.

So do regimental ties.

King's Own Yorkshire Light Infantry

Royal Artillery

Duke of Atholl

In the last two wars it became customary for larger bodies of troops to mark their corporate identity by the use of formation signs, often designed by one of H.M. heralds.

The Lincolnshire Regiment

Scottish Horse, raised by Atholl

7th Armoured Division, [the "Desert Rats"]

The spirit of a corps—with its continuing service and loyalty to the Queen—is embodied in its Colours, which are specially consecrated before presentation to the Regiment. In addition to the actual Colours, there are often flags bearing company or squadron badges.

Queen's Standard of Royal Horse Guards [the Blues]

Certain troops, including the Household Cavalry and Foot Guards, form a permanent part of the Queen's household, and are called the Household Brigade. Their badges are usually drawn from the royal badges or from the stars of the noble orders of knighthood.

Company Colour, Queen's Company Grenadier Guards

HER MAJESTY'S HOUSEHOLD

ost of the Great Officers of Her Majesty's Household are entitled to special heraldic insignia by virtue of their service, for it is the highest honour to be allowed to serve the Queen, who is the living symbol of all her peoples.

Earl Marshal of England

Lord High Steward of Ireland

Chief Butler of Ireland

Some place the insignia of their office behind their shield.

Other officers of the Queen add a special quartering for their office—or have a special badge.

Lord High Constable of Scotland

Royal Banner Bearer of Scotland

The Honourable the Queen's Champion of England

Badge of the Queen's Champion

PART FIVE

ARMS AND THE RULES

AUTHORITY OVER ARMS

B ecause disputes arose over coats of arms, the King gave authority to certain Great Officers to judge in such matters— and also to stop men from assuming heraldic honours to which they were not entitled.

Howard, Duke of Norfolk, Earl Marshal of England

In England, this authority was given to the Lord High Constable (when there was one) and to the Earl Marshal—who is also the Duke of Norfolk

In Scotland, the authority was given to the High Sennachie, who became styled the Lord Lyon King of Arms from the lion in the Scottish royal coat.

Today, legal control of armorial rights is still vested in the Court of the Earl Marshal, for England, and in the Court of the Lord Lyon, for Scotland.

Lord Lyon King of Arms

These Great Officers were also made responsible for recording genealogies and organising public ceremonies—the traditional function of a herald.

48

HERALDS

To assist them, these Great Officers have therefore the services of a number of officers of arms, generally known as "heralds".

In England, the Principal King of Arms is called Garter. There are also two other Kings of Arms called Clarenceux and Norroy, six Heralds and four Pursuivants, who with Garter form collectively the College of Arms under the Earl Marshal.

In Scotland, there are three Heralds and three Pursuivants, who with other officials make up the Court of the Lord Lyon.

The Republic of Eire has appointed a Principal Herald of Ireland : and Norroy as Ulster King of Arms deals with Northern Ireland's heraldry.

Eagle Pursuivant of the Earl of Derby

Great nobles also had their private officers of arms, and some still maintain the right.

Slains Pursuivant of the Earl of Erroll

Heralds also made proclamations, and carried out diplomatic missions. Since they publicly represented their masters in the performance of these duties, they wore their masters' coats.

Duke of Brittany

Duke of Bourbon

As the use of arms developed, heralds evolved practical conventions governing the design and arrangement of coats of arms. These conventions make up the Science of Heraldry.

"TINCTURES"

Only five colours are in general use in heraldry—red (called "gules"), blue ("azure"), black ("sable"), green ("vert") and purple ("purpure").

d'Albret

Maienthal

Gournay

de Menezes

Pupellin

Aubert

Zgraia

There are also two metals used—gold ("or") and silver ("argent"), often depicted yellow and white—

and a number of furs, including ermine (white stoat with black tails), "contre-ermine" (black with white tails), "erminois" (gold with black tails) and "vair" (alternate blue and white squirrel skins).

Duke of
Brittany

de
Rousselet

Van der
Eze

Zu
Pappenheim

Some families have plain shields, but usually some "charge" is placed upon the background or "field". Normally colour is not placed on another colour, nor metal on metal, as being too indistinct at a distance. But colour shows up well on metal, and metal on colour.

"ORDINARIES"

Certain charges called "ordinaries", which sometimes have diminutives of their own, include

the *chief*—

Menzies

the *saltire*—

Fitz Gerald

the *Cross*,
which has many variations,
like "cross-crosslet fitchée"—

Burke

Rattray

the *fess* (fasce),
which can be reduced
to form a bar or *bars*—

Melville

Harcourt

the *pale*,
which can be diminished
into *palets*—

Schönstein

**Count
of Foix**

the *chevron*,
which can also be
diminished—

Trelawney

Richelieu

the *pile*,
which can be multiplied
to form "passion nails"—

Chandos

Anstruther

the *bordure*—and the *bend* (bande),
a diagonal line from the
"dexter" top corner of the shield,

("dexter" is right and "sinister" left
as you shelter behind the shield).

Hundescote

Scrope

A diagonal line the other way is a *bend sinister*, in French
a "barre", which is not necessarily a mark of illegitimacy.

Barre

"SUB-ORDINARIES"

Other ordinaries or "sub-ordinaries" include

the *quarter*,
    which when reduced
        is called the *canton*—

Dasbourg

Sutton

the *pairle* (pall), which is
    sometimes cut or "couped"
       to form a "shake-fork"—

von Rüpplin

Cunningham

the *escutcheon*,
    which is often "voided"
    by having its centre cut out—

Wavrin

Baliol

the *lozenge* :
when voided they are often
          called *mascles*—
and can also be narrowed into
fusils—

Schwerin

Rohan

        the *gyron*—

Percy

de Cluseau

roundels (often given
separate names for
each tincture)—
        rings or *annulets*—

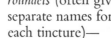

Courtenay

Musgrave

billets—

      flaunches (flanks)—

Beaumanoir

Martinet

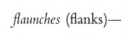

the *label*,
usually mark of an heir
(or sometimes a
disinherited line)—and the *fret*.

Van
Oostenwolde

Maltravers

"LINES OF PARTITION"

But often coats have no charge, the field itself being divided into two or more tinctures. Thus it can be parted

Count of Stockau

per *fess*—

per *pale*—

Waldegrave

Capponi

per *bend*—

per *saltire*—

Von Hartzheim

Aston

per *chevron*—   or *quarterly*.

Hohenzollern

If the shield is divided into three it is *tierced*. For example,

Vendramini

"tierced in fess",
   or "tierced in pairle reversed".

Von Haldermanstetten

There can also be a number of equal divisions, such as

Grey, Earl of Stamford

barry of six—

fretty—

Bellew

Warenne

chequy—   or *gyronny*.

Campbell

The outlines, too, can be varied in such ways as

Sinclair

a Cross *engrailed*—
   per bend *embattled*—

Boyle, Earl of Cork

La Poer

a chief *indented*—
   a fess *dancetty*—

West

Drummond of Megginch

per fess *wavy*—
   or barry *nebuly* of six.

Blount

53

FLORA AND FAUNA

The whole zoo and garden are drawn on for heraldic "devices".

Oliver Cromwell

The lion, unless otherwise stated, is *rampant*. Looking backwards it is rear *reguardant*.

Pryse of Gogerddan

Strange

Walking, it is *passant*. Lions *guardant* (looking towards you) become "leopards".

Ogilvy

Crest of Laird of Moncreiffe

Halved, a lion becomes a *demi*-lion. Parts torn off are *erased* : thus "a boar's head erased".

Crest of Duke of Argyll

Windisch-Grätz

Parts cut off are *couped* : thus "a wolf's head couped". Facing and neckless, heads are *cabossed* : thus "a hart's head cabossed".

Mackenzie

Lord Northbourne

Dolphins are usually *embowed* (arched). *Vorant* creatures devour : thus "a serpent crowned vorant a child".

Visconti

Ramsay

Eagles are usually *displayed* (wings spread). The *martlet*, a conventional bird, has no legs (and abroad neither beak nor tail)

Arundell

de Trafford

There are many fantastic creatures such as the *griffin*. Such flowers as the rose may be *barbed* and *seeded* of different tinctures.

Lippe

Lilly of Stoke Prior

With a bit of stalk, they are *slipped* : "a lily slipped" is very different from the conventional *fleur-de-lys*.

Digby

54

OTHER DEVICES

Other devices have been chosen from every conceivable source.

The *sun* has many rays.

The horns of *crescents* point upwards, otherwise they are *increscent* or *decrescent*.

The *estoile* usually has six wavy rays.
The molet or *mullet* usually has five points ; when pierced it forms a "spur-rowel".

The *escallop* shell (badge of pilgrimage)—

the broad-arrow or *pheon*—

the *maunch* or sleeve—

the wheatsheaf or *garb*—

water-bougets (skin bags for water)—

trefoils, *quatrefoils* and *cinquefoils* —are all much used.

Modern industry has added to the devices in use. Devices shown in their natural colours are said to be *proper*.

Earldom of Lothian

Oliphant

Ingilby

Murray

Crest of Jardine of Applegirth

Pringle

Sidney

Hastings

Grosvenor

de Ros

Livingstone

Borough of Swindon

Wellwood

CANTING ARMS

The devices on *canting* coats make puns on their owners' names.

Cockburn

Breakspear

ADDED CHARGES

La Tremouille

C harges can be varied or combined in innumerable ways—on plain or parti-coloured fields.

La Rochefoucauld

Field Marshal Alexander

Tinctures reversed on either side of a partition line are *counter-changed.*

Mackenzie of Glenmuick

Beaumont

The field is sometimes strewn or *semée* with small charges.

Sometimes charges are added to an existing coat because of some famous feat—

Douglas

Kennedy

or because of a royal connection (in Scotland often by grant of the "royal tressure").

Kennedy augmented

King of Scots

Such additions, made by special grant of the Sovereign, are called *augmentations.*

Howard

The "Flodden Augmentation"

Howard augmented

How Howard got his augmentation

BLAZONING

To "blazon" a coat of arms is to describe it in technical terms, in order to be brief yet precise. This is done in an accepted sequence:

First name the field—	then the principal charge—	then lesser charges on the field—	then lesser devices on the principal charge.
Argent,	*on a chevron Gules,*	*between three leopard's faces Sable,*	*three castles Or.*

de Sausmarez

Chiefs and cantons, with any devices on them, are mentioned later, and bordures come last of all.

Thus : "argent two barrulets [narrow bars] wavy azure, between in chief two maple leaves slipped and in base a thistle eradicated [uprooted] gules, a bordure sable charged with eight bezants".

Lord Beaverbrook

Quarterings are numbered and blazoned consecutively:

Quarterly, ... *1st and 4th, Or,* .... *a fess chequy Azure and Argent,* .... *within a royal tressure Gules,* .... *2nd and 3rd, Argent,* .... *a lion Azure.*

Crichton-Stuart

57

HEADGEAR

Shields are often "ensigned" with official headgear of rank, set immediately above the shield.

Monarchs have closed *crowns*.

King of England

Peers have open *coronets*.

Earl of Home

Lochiel

Scots feudal barons have *chapeaux*, which all peers too may wear inside their coronets.

Duke of Devonshire

Archbishop of York

Bishops and abbots have their *mitres*— and all clergy have clerical *hats* coloured and tasselled according to their degree.

Minister of the Kirk of Holyroodhouse

Burgh of Bervie

Scots burghs have *mural coronets*—and Scottish county councils have a special green coronet with wheatsheaves.

Midlothian County Council

Above the coronet or hat is placed the helmet, which differs in metal and design according to rank.

Royalty	Peers	Knights	Scots Barons and Chiefs	Gentlemen
Gold, with bars	Silver, gold bars	Steel, visor open	Tournament helm	Steel, closed

Crest of Douglas Fairbanks, Jnr.

Crests normally issue from *wreaths*, but there are exceptions.   For example, some Scots chiefs and old English families use *crest-coronets*—

Crest of Earl De la Warr

Crest of Duke of Northumberland

some Scots barons and old English families use *chapeaux*, and some distinguished naval families use *naval crowns*.

Crest of Earl Jellicoe

INSIGNIA

O fficials are often entitled to place their insignia of office behind their shield.

Hereditary Keeper of St. Fillan's Crozier

Sir Victor Fortune, K.B.E., C.B.,D.S.O.

Holders of collars of SS and members of knightly orders may add their badge and collar, Garter, circlet or riband to their achievement. Decorations may be suspended by their ribbons below the shield.

Similarly, baronets may hang their badge from its riband—or the badge may be charged on the shield itself (in a canton or inescutcheon)—or even both.

Sir Edward Malet, Baronet.

SUPPORTERS

City of Perth

In England, hereditary supporters are allowed only to peers—in Scotland they are allowed to chiefs and to certain ancient barons as well. But some institutions have supporters—and, for instance, Knights of the Garter, the Thistle, and Knights Grand Cross of other orders are granted them for life.

Usually there is a supporter on either side of the shield, but sometimes the shield is borne by a single supporter.

Supporters usually stand on a grassy compartment, but very few families have special compartments.

Dundas of that Ilk

"SEIZE QUARTIERS"

4th Duke of Buccleuch married the Hon. Harriet Townshend

Marquess of Bath married the Hon. Isabella Byng

Viscount Hamilton married Lady Harriet Douglas

Duke of Bedford married Lady Georgiana Gordon

Earl of Bradford married Miss Moncreiffe of Moncreiffe

Lord Forester married Lady Mary Manners

Frederick Lumley married Miss Charlotte Beresford

Andrew Drummond married Lady Elizabeth Manners

When his two parents, four grandparents, eight great-grandparents, and all sixteen great-great-grandparents had coats of arms, a man is said to have *seize quartiers.*

"Seize Quartiers" of the 8th Duke of Buccleuch

Of course this has nothing to do with quartering, as none of the women need to be heraldic heiresses.

60

PART SIX

ARMS AND
YOU

YOUR OWN ARMS

IF YOU ARE ENGLISH, OR OF ENGLISH DESCENT, you are entitled to arms if you can prove your male descent (father to son) from someone whose coat is officially recorded at the College of Arms, Queen Victoria Street, London EC4V 4BT.

To add to these records the names of any of the intervening generations down to yourself costs one or two guineas.

If you are a younger son, or belong to a younger branch, you must remember to "difference" the plain arms of your ancestor.

But if you have not (or cannot prove) such a descent, you may apply to the Earl Marshal through the College of Arms for Letters Patent granting you special arms of your own.

This costs £530, as it entails a considerable amount of expert knowledge on the part of the heralds, and also includes the cost of preparing the beautifully illuminated patent. Moreover, neither the College nor its officers receive any subsidy from public funds, and its building and records have to be maintained from their fees.

Such Letters Patent entitle you and your descendants to arms for ever.

YOUR OWN ARMS

IF YOU ARE SCOTS, OR OF SCOTTISH DESCENT, you are entitled to arms if you can prove you are the heir of someone who has recorded arms in Lyon Register, which began in 1672 and is kept in the Court of the Lord Lyon, H.M. New Register House, Princes Street, Edinburgh EH1 3YT. You may still register ancient arms if legally proved heir to someone who bore them before 1672.

If you are a younger son, or belong to a younger branch, you are still entitled to arms, but must apply to the Lord Lyon for a suitable "difference" to be "matriculated" for you in Lyon Register. This costs about £80–made up of fees (which go direct to H.M. Treasury) and the cost of the Herald Painter's work on the illuminated parchment.

But if you have not (or cannot prove) such a descent, you may apply to the Lord Lyon King of Arms at his Court for Letters Patent granting you special arms of your own.

This costs about £280, made up as before of Treasury Fees and the cost of painting the title deed itself.

This entitles you and your descendants to arms for ever, though younger sons must of course "matriculate" their particular differences.

These arms are protected for you by all the force of the Law of Scotland (where the use of bogus arms is illegal) and anyone who infringes your patent will be prevented from doing so, and may be prosecuted and fined by Lyon Court.

63

FINIS